ARCTIC WHALES
& WHALING

**Bobbie Kalman
& Ken Faris**

The Arctic World Series

Crabtree Publishing Company

The Arctic World Series
Created by Bobbie Kalman

Editor-in-Chief:
Bobbie Kalman

Writing team:
Bobbie Kalman
Janine Schaub
Susan Hughes
Tilly Crawley
Christine Arthurs
Ken Faris

Managing Editor:
Janine Schaub

Editors:
Tilly Crawley
Christine Arthurs
Susan Hughes
Shaun Oakey

Design:
Heather Delfino
Maureen Shaughnessy
Stephen Latimer

Computer layout:
Christine Arthurs

Map: Chrismar Mapping Service

Printer:
Bryant Press

For the Pokiak family
in Tuktoyaktuk

Special thanks to: Ken Faris for his photographs of the Tuktoyaktuk whale hunt; the Pokiaks for their hospitality during Ken's visit; Robin Brass for his desktop publishing advice and linotronic output; Arnie Krause for his continuing patience and support.

Cataloguing in Publication Data

Kalman, Bobbie, 1947-
    Arctic whales and whaling

(The Arctic world series)
Includes index.
ISBN 0-86505-146-1 (bound) ISBN 0-86505-156-9 (pbk.)
1.Whales - Arctic regions - Juvenile literature.
2. Whaling - Arctic regions - Juvenile literature. 3. Whaling - Arctic regions - History - Juvenile literature, I. Faris, Ken 1956 -. II. Title. III. Series: Kalman, Bobbie, 1947- . The Arctic world series.

QL737.C4K34 1988   j599.5'

350 Fifth Avenue
Suite 3308
New York
N.Y. 10118

120 Carlton Street
Suite 309
Toronto, Ontario
Canada M5A 4K2

Contents

Whales

Do whales really talk to one another the way people do? We now know that they make a whole variety of noises underwater and that each species has its own language, but until recently hardly anything was known about whales. You can imagine how difficult it is to study animals that live beneath the water and are often on the move. In the past the only way scientists could learn about whales was by examining their carcasses.

Now, thanks to scientific inventions such as the hydrophone and the observations of dedicated marine biologists, researchers are able to study and record the activities of whales in their natural environment. We are beginning to know more about these gigantic, intelligent creatures.

Not many left

Once, great numbers of whales swam in all the oceans of the world. Today there are scarcely any whales left. In less than four hundred years all the waters once inhabited by whales have been emptied of one species after another. In the last fifty years over two million whales have been killed. Some species of whales are in danger of disappearing altogether!

Arctic Whales and Whaling is about the whales that live in the Arctic year round, the whalers who hunted them for profit, and the Inuit who depended, and still depend, on whales for food. This book describes the history of whaling and its tragic results. It is a sad tale not only for the whales, but also for the people who depend on them for food and necessities.

Saving the whale

The story of the whale is not, however, a hopeless one. Concerned people around the world are working to save arctic whales. As well as studying the ways of whales, these people have brought the serious plight of whales to public attention. The more we know about whales, the greater the chances are that we can prevent them from becoming extinct. You can help make sure there is a future for whales by learning about them and passing your knowledge on to others.

From land to sea

Whales are the largest creatures in the world. In fact, the largest whale, the blue whale, is the biggest creature ever known to have lived!

Many people think of whales as big fish, but whales are mammals, just as we are. Millions of years ago the ancestors of whales lived on land. It is hard to imagine, but these early creatures had nostrils, hair, and legs.

Whales started living in water about sixty million years ago. No one is sure why this happened. Over time different species of whales developed. Although the whales of today look different from their ancestors, they are still mammals.

Whales had to adapt in many ways to their new lives in the water. Like all mammals, they obtain oxygen from the air. Whales cannot breathe the oxygen in water the way fish do because they do not have gills. Whales breathe by means of lungs.

Breathe in, blow out

What used to be nostrils in the ancestors of whales slowly developed into one or two blowholes located at the top of the whale's head. The word "blowhole" gives the false idea that whales only use their blowholes to let out air. In fact, whales inhale and exhale through their blowholes.

How do they do it?

Blowholes allow a whale to breathe without lifting more than a small part of its head out of the water. When the whale breathes out, the used air in its lungs is released with a whooshing sound. This exhaled air is much warmer than the air above the water. The cooler outside air turns the whale's breath to steam, just as it makes your breath visible on a cold day. When the whale exhales, water close to its blowhole is pushed into the air, creating a natural water fountain. People can spot and even identify a whale by this column of steam and spray, for each species has a different spout.

Take a deep breath!

Most whales remain underwater for about ten minutes between blows. Whales that search for their food deep in the ocean, however, can remain under the water from twenty to sixty minutes, if necessary. Whales are able to breathe less often and hold their breath longer than we can because their muscles, blood, heart, and lungs have become very efficient at using and storing oxygen.

A whale of a mammal

Whales changed in shape and size when they moved into the sea. If the largest whales were to now live on land, their bones would break under the pressure of their great bulk. It is the sea that has enabled whales to grow to the sizes they are today. Have you ever noticed that you seem to weigh less in water than out of water? We are able to float in water because water helps support our weight. Water helps support the huge mass of a whale in exactly the same way.

The tail end

Over millions of years a whale's arms and legs slowly developed into flippers and a tail. Its wide tail became two flexible flukes. One third of the whale's body is strong muscle. These changes have made this mammal into a powerful swimmer. When a blue whale swims at top speed, it can easily keep up with a modern ship.

Staying warm

A layer of fat, called blubber, keeps the whale warm. Just as a home has insulation inside its walls and beneath its roof, a whale locks in its body heat beneath its blubber. If it gets too hot, its body heat can escape through its flippers and tail flukes, which are not insulated. The smoothness of blubber also helps streamline a whale so it is able to glide more easily through water.

Where whales live

Whales are found throughout the oceans of the world. Some whales spend all year in the warm waters close to the equator. Others spend their summers in polar seas, feeding on the plankton that thrive there in the late spring and summer. When winter comes, these whales migrate to warmer seas to give birth to calves.

Types of whales

There are two types of whales: toothed and toothless. Of the ninety-two whale species, eighty are toothed. Toothed whales do not chew their food; they swallow it whole. They use their teeth to catch and hold their prey. They eat mainly the fish and squid that live in the lower depths of the ocean. One reason for the relatively small size of toothed whales may be that their food supply is more limited than that of the toothless whales. Of all the toothed whales, only the sperm whale has grown to a really large size.

Long plates of baleen hang from a whale's upper jawbone.

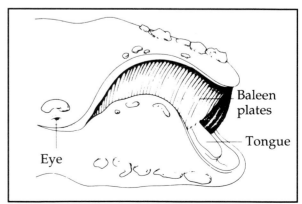

Baleen whales

Toothless whales catch abundant, tiny ocean organisms, such as krill, in their baleen. Some whales have as many as four hundred triangular baleen plates hanging from their upper jaws. Baleen looks like a rough, hairy mat and functions as a sieve to trap food. It is made of keratin, the same material as that of horns and fingernails. Because baleen makes feeding an easy task, baleen whales grow to be very large.

Rorquals and right whales

There are two types of baleen whales: rorquals and right whales. Rorquals, also called fin whales, have a well-defined triangular fin near their tails; right whales do not. When a rorqual whale blows, its spout is pear shaped because it comes from one blowhole. When a right whale blows, the spout is V shaped because there are two blowholes.

Feeding in gulps

Although both rorquals and right whales have baleen, they feed in different ways. Pleats, or grooves, in the rorqual's throat enable it to hold a great quantity of water at one time. The rorqual takes a huge gulp of water filled with ocean creatures, closes its mouth, and squirts the water out through its short baleen. It then swallows the food left behind in its mouth.

Feeding by sifting

Right whales swim with their mouths held open, letting the water flow through the long curtain of baleen. Krill, plankton, and fish get trapped in the baleen as the water sifts through. Then the whales close their mouths, spit out a small amount of water, and swallow their food. Unlike rorquals, right whales do not have grooves. Instead, their baleen is longer, so their catch is greater.

A cross section of a baleen whale's head showing how baleen whales feed.

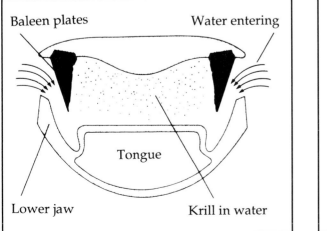

Baleen plates — Water entering — Tongue — Lower jaw — Krill in water

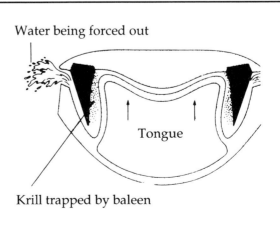

Water being forced out — Tongue — Krill trapped by baleen

Whale sizes

On the following pages you will learn about the three whales that live in the Arctic year round. Other whales travel to the Arctic in summer to feed in its plentiful waters. Some of these whales are shown on the chart on this page, while others are illustrated on pages 12 and 13.

Blue whale

The largest whale of all, this rorqual's sole food is krill. The blue whale ranges throughout the oceans of the world. It migrates south to calve and north to feed in the polar waters during the summer.

Fin whale

The fin whale gets its name from the tall fin on its back. It is the second-largest whale in the world. This rorqual lives in deep waters and feeds on krill, crustaceans, and a wide variety of fish.

Sperm whale

The sperm whale is the largest toothed whale. It can be identified by its huge block-shaped head. The sperm whale gets its name from a special oil-filled space in its head called the spermaceti organ. Although there are many theories, no one is certain what this organ's true function is.

Blue whale

Fin whale

Sperm whale

Humpback whale

Minke whale

Orca

Northern bottlenose whale

Beluga

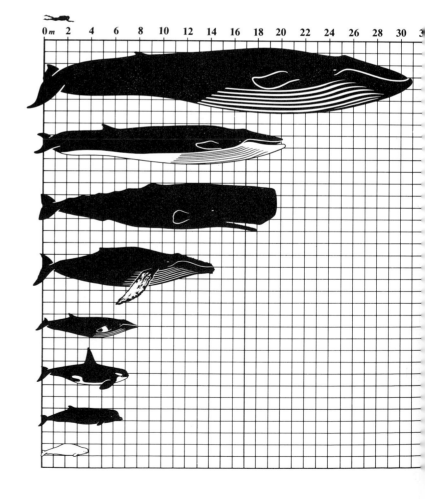

Humpback whale

A humpback is easy to recognize because its flippers are longer than those of any other whale. Unlike other rorquals, it has strange bumps on its head. It is covered in more barnacles and whale lice than other whales. The humpback is famous for its long, sad-sounding songs.

Minke whale

The minke is the smallest rorqual whale. It ranges throughout the oceans of the world, traveling as far north as the edge of the polar ice pack.

Orca

The striking black-and-white orca is a member of the dolphin family. It is the only member of this family that eats warm-blooded animals.

Northern bottlenose whale

A member of the beaked toothed-whale family, the northern bottlenose has a small snout and flat forehead. It lives in the arctic waters of the Atlantic Ocean during the summer and migrates as far south as the Mediterranean Sea.

Gray whale

Gray whales are different from all other baleen whales. They have many barnacles, very short baleen, and only two to four throat grooves. These huge whales feed by plowing through the sediment at the bottom of the ocean. Grays are best known for their incredible migrations. In one year many gray whales travel from the Arctic to Mexico and back—a trip of over 19 000 kilometers!

The northern right whale

Perhaps only four hundred northern right whales are left in the world! Although these whales have been protected from whaling for fifty years, their chances of survival are not very promising!

Arctic residents and visitors

The three species that remain in the Arctic all year are the narwhal, beluga, and bowhead. Two of these whales are toothed, and one is a baleen whale. Find the three arctic residents and identify the other whales you have already read about on the previous two pages.

1. Humpback whale
2. Bowhead whale
3. Northern right whale
4. Narwhal
5. Beluga
6. Blue whale
7. Minke whale
8. Sperm whale
9. Gray whale

a bowhead nursing

Arctic whales

The bowhead whale

The bowhead is a large black whale with a splotch of white on its chin and belly. For hundreds of years it was the favorite of whalers because of its large baleen and thick blubber. Known first as the Greenland right whale, its name was changed to bowhead because its enormous curved head reminded whalers of a giant bow.

The bowhead lives only in arctic waters. Western arctic bowheads live in the Bering Sea and spend their summers in the Beaufort Sea area. Eastern arctic bowheads winter in the open waters of the Davis Strait and off the west coast of Greenland. They occasionally go as far south as Labrador. In summer they can be found in Lancaster Sound, Davis Strait, and in the northern Hudson Bay.

The bowhead has been hunted almost to extinction. Today only around 3000 live in the western Arctic, and there are only a few hundred in the eastern Arctic.

The beluga

"Beluga" is a Russian word meaning white. Belugas are small toothed whales that often travel in pods. Baby belugas change color as they grow up. They are born brown and become a yellowish gray color before turning white at four or five years of age. The white helps them blend into the snow and ice of their arctic environment.

In summer belugas live in the shallow bays and inlets of the Arctic Ocean. In winter ice forces them to move into deeper and more open waters. Belugas are able to stay in the icy sea water because as much as forty percent of their bodies is blubber. To build up and maintain such a large store of fat, these whales must constantly search for food. The arctic cod is the beluga's favorite meal, but it will eat almost anything—even sea worms if that is the only food available.

Belugas are nicknamed "sea canaries" because of their great variety of trills, moos, clicks, and squeaks. Their flexible

14

faces allow them to make different facial expressions. If you came face to face with a beluga, you would probably think it was smiling at you!

The narwhal

The narwhal, also known as the "unicorn of the sea," is famous for its long, spiral tusk. This tusk is really not a tusk at all, but a tooth. The tooth on the left of the jaw cuts through the upper lip and keeps growing until it becomes a tusk. It spirals counter-clockwise towards the tip and can grow to a length of three meters. Occasionally the tooth on the right side also grows into a tusk. Most male narwhals have tusks, but some females have them too. No one is sure why these tusks exist. They are far too brittle to be used as weapons or tools. Some scientists believe that the narwhal with the longest tusk may get to mate with the most females.

A long tusk is important to a male narwhal but, unfortunately, it is also valuable to its hunters. Narwhal tusks can be sold for large sums of money. Perhaps people buy narwhal tusks in the hope of possessing some unicorn magic!

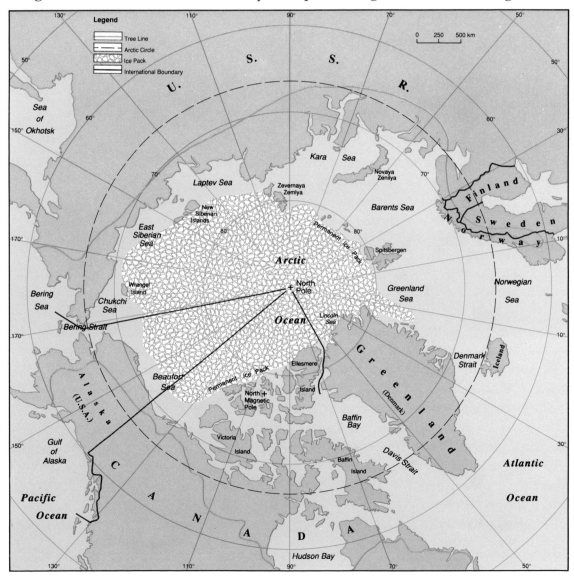

Fascinating whale facts

Whale watchers

The more people find out about whales, the more they realize how friendly, intelligent, and fascinating these gentle mammals are. In the last few years whale watching has become a popular pastime. In fact, whale watching is now a major tourist attraction. There are special whale-watching locations that offer spectacular views of whales swimming along their migration routes. On the west coast alone more than fifty tours and cruises are available for those who want to be sure that they are in the right place at the right time.

What kinds of activities can whale watchers hope to see? One observer reported two narwhals crossing their tusks above the water as if they were dueling with swords. He also said that he saw large groups of these whales dive exactly at the same time as if they were a single, gigantic animal. Another whale watcher was introduced to a baby whale by its mother. She pushed the baby above the water for a breath of air and a quick greeting. Whale watchers claim to have a whale of a time on these outings!

Yummy!

People who have tried whale milk say that it tastes like a mixture of oil, milk of magnesia, liver, and fish! Humans may hate the flavor, but baby whales thrive on it. A baby blue whale drinks over five hundred liters of its mother's milk each day. Drinking this fat-rich beverage allows the animal to gain weight at a tremendous rate—approximately four kilograms an hour!

A free ride

When a baby whale has a full stomach, it often gets sleepy. Even though it may snooze by its mother's side, it does not get left behind as she speeds away. The water passing between the mother and calf helps carry the baby along.

Spy hopping

What is a whale doing when it is "spy-hopping?" Migrating whales raise their heads out of the water to have a look around. Scientists believe that whales are searching for landmarks along the coast to help them find their way north or south.

Whale whiskers?

A characteristic of all mammals is the presence of hair on the body. Even though whales are classified as mammals, adults are often hairless. Whales have a few whiskers when they are born, but these hairs usually fall out shortly after birth!

Built-in radar

Whales send out hundreds of clicking sounds into the water. When one of these sound waves reaches an object, it bounces off it and comes back towards the whale. The time that it takes for the echo of the click to return tells the whale about the shape, size, and location of the object. This ability to locate objects by using sound waves is called echolocation. It is also used by another mammal—the bat!

Munch a bunch of krill

If you wanted to satisfy a whale of an appetite, you might have to eat a mountain of food. A blue whale requires over nine hundred kilograms of krill to feel full!

Opera singers

Some whales make underwater squeaks, cries, whistles, moans, and rumbles. Many scientists believe that each whale sings a unique song and uses its voice to communicate with other whales. These songs carry for many kilometers under the ocean, allowing whales to talk to one another over great distances. Some researchers feel that the songs of the humpback whale are as complicated as our operas. Many songs take over a half hour to sing. If the whale is interrupted, it will later pick up the tune where it left off. Long passages of certain songs may even be passed from generation to generation of whales.

I can sing better than you can!

It has been observed by scientists that humpback whales, the most talented of singing whales, compete for the companionship of certain females by singing their best songs. If there is not a clear winner, the competing males may wallop each other with mighty swats of their huge tails. Take that!

The early whalers

The history of whaling begins in the Stone Age. Evidence from cave drawings many thousands of years old show that porpoises and dolphins were hunted even then. Native peoples of the Arctic have been hunting whales for so long that whaling has become a basic part of their cultures.

Native arctic whaling

The Chukchi of Russia and the Inuit of Alaska, Greenland, and Canada all depended on the whale for their food, clothing, shelter, and equipment. These native peoples hunted only the number of whales necessary to feed themselves and their families.

The native people used every bit of the whale. The meat and organs of the animal fed them, and the blubber with the skin still attached, called *muktuk*, supplied them with a source of many essential vitamins, including A, D, and especially C. Native people could not get enough vitamin C from vegetables because there was no way to grow them in the harsh climate.

Besides being an important source of nourishment, blubber was boiled down into oil for stone lamps. The ribs of the whales were used for house rafters, and the jaw bones as sled runners. Vertebrae made stools, and shoulder blades were fashioned into snow shovels. The tough, elastic baleen of some whales became fish lines and nets, harpoon lashings, knife blades, and carved toys for children.

Hunting weapons

Harpoons were made out of bone or tusk. The tip of the harpoon was of ivory or antler, attached to a line made from sealskin. Harpoons were used to spear the whale and hold it with a line, but the final kill was made with a lance. The tip of the lance was long, slender, and carved from stone. It had to be strong and sharp enough to go through the whale's thick layer of blubber and puncture a vital organ.

Each hunter carried harpoons, a long line, an inflated sealskin, a lance, a pointed tube, and a knife. If he was chasing a whale that did not have a thick layer of blubber, such as a narwhal, he used the tube to blow air into the whale's stomach so that it would float after it was killed. The knife was taken along in case the whale got entangled in the harpoon line and overturned the boat. In that case, the hunter had to cut the line quickly to save his own life.

Floats

About one thousand years ago the Inuit began using floats made from sealskin. A seal's insides were pulled through its mouth opening, leaving the skin behind. All openings were then tied off, and a piece of ivory or wood was plugged into the mouth of the carcass. When the float was needed, the mouthpiece was removed and the skin inflated.

Floats were attached by a line to the tip of the harpoon. When the harpoon pierced the whale, the tip and line came away from the harpoon shaft and remained in the whale. The attached floats did not allow the whale to dive very deeply. The float created a drag in the water, which slowed down and tired out the harpooned whale.

Once the whale was finally killed, the floats kept the carcass from sinking and allowed the hunters to keep track of the whale in the water.

Hunting by kayak

Small whales were usually hunted from long, narrow, canoe-like boats called kayaks. These skin-covered boats had one, and sometimes two, seating holes.

Kayakers hunted in groups; few Inuit hunted alone. A kayak could easily become entangled in the harpoon line and overturn. In that case, the second kayaker could save the first by grabbing onto the man's floating trousers and hauling him aboard.

A favorite tactic by a group of hunters was to form a line behind a pod of belugas and then herd the whales towards shallow water by slapping paddles on the surface of the water. The nervous belugas fled from the sound, only to become trapped between the shore and the boats.

Although most kayaks had one or two holes, this Alaskan Inupiat shows his model of a three-holed kayak made at the request of Russian traders. A full-sized kayak was built to seat one Russian between two Inupiat paddlers.

In search of the whale

Narrow straits were excellent places for kayakers to find narwhals or belugas. A kayaker silently followed the wake of a whale as it swam just under the surface of the water. He waited for the whale to blow and then paddled quickly to close in on the animal. He harpooned the whale once, and then again when it rose a second time. The floats attached to the harpooned whale eventually tired out the animal. When the whale was exhausted, the hunter then killed it with several thrusts of his lance.

Hunting in umiaks

Larger whales were hunted in bigger boats that held up to eight whalers. These large boats were called umiaks. In the spring the whalers hauled their umiaks across long stretches of ice. When they found cracks in the ice, they watched the water for migrating whales. As soon as the whales were spotted, a team of men leapt into their umiak and sped towards the whales.

Six men paddled, the harpooner shouted out directions, and the helmsman helped steer the boat by operating a small rudder at the back of the umiak. Once a whale surfaced and was harpooned, the lines and the floats were quickly drawn into the water by the fleeing whale. The crew manoeuvered the umiak away from the speared whale so that when the whale's tail came up, it would not overturn the boat.

Towing in the whale

A whale was often killed far from land, and several umiaks were needed to tow the animal towards shore. Ivory toggles were used to hold the whale's fins close to its body. Tying the fins down in this way prevented unnecessary dragging while the whale was being towed. When the whale was finally brought in, everyone helped cut it up. Butchering a whale was a social occasion. The whale was divided in the order that the men "touched" or harpooned it. The first harpooner cut a piece out of the whale's forehead to show that he was the first. He then got the biggest share, followed by the other harpooners whose shares matched the order in which they touched the whale. Everyone got something.

Although the Inuit women did not take part in the actual killing of the whale, they helped with all the chores. They sewed new clothes for the hunt and helped get the chase under way. After the hunt the women cut up the whale and prepared the meat and muktuk. Men, women, and children alike took part in the festivities after the kill.

Part of the Inuit culture

In many northern communities the Inuit depended on whales for their very survival. These magnificent beasts were treated with great respect. Ceremonies were often held before and after a whale hunt as a way of showing appreciation for these much-valued creatures.

A time for celebration

On the day the hunt was completed, the native hunters usually held a party, or in some communities, a whale festival. It was a celebration of thanksgiving. The celebrations included dances, games, and feasts. The blanket toss was a favorite event. Crew members stood in a circle holding the edges of a hide. They tossed the captain in it. If he tried to stand up, they tried to make him lose his balance. Then each crew member took a turn as the villagers watched, cheered, and laughed. In some arctic communities whaling celebrations are still carried out in similar ways today.

Whaling boats and tools

The boats and implements on this page were used in native whaling. They have been drawn to scale. The ulu and toggles have also been magnified to show detail.

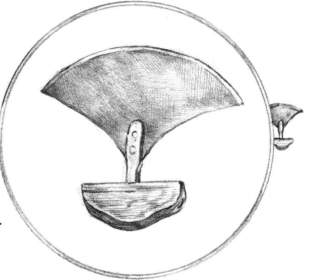

The ulu was used for butchering the whale. It was sharpened with a stone.

Whale hunting was usually done from umiaks. Umiaks could hold several hunters.

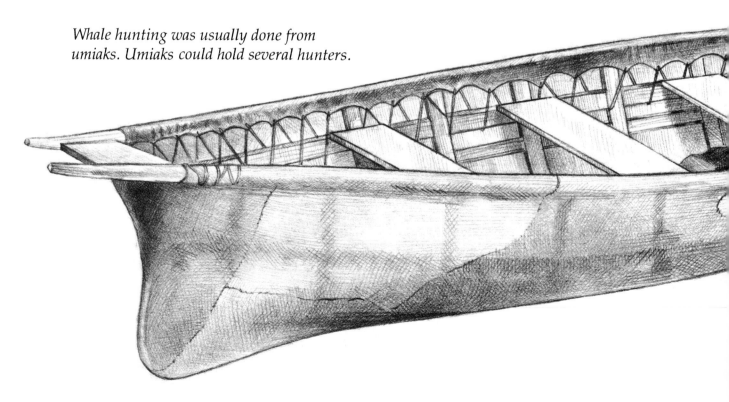

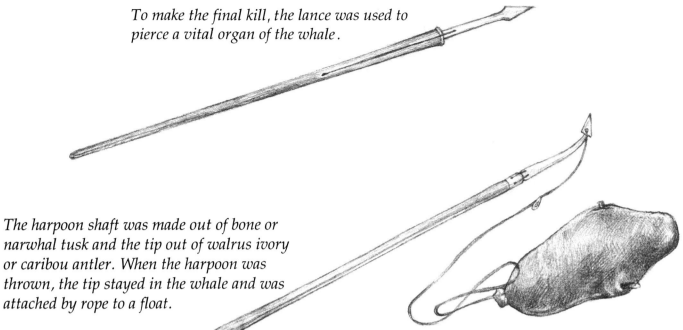

To make the final kill, the lance was used to pierce a vital organ of the whale.

The harpoon shaft was made out of bone or narwhal tusk and the tip out of walrus ivory or caribou antler. When the harpoon was thrown, the tip stayed in the whale and was attached by rope to a float.

A float made from a seal slowed down the wounded whale and kept it from diving too deeply.

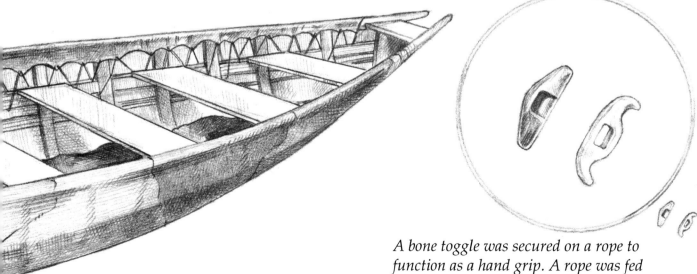

A bone toggle was secured on a rope to function as a hand grip. A rope was fed through the hole in the toggle and tied on either side, making the rope much easier to manage.

Kayaks had either one or two holes.

A whale hunt in Tuktoyaktuk

Tuktoyaktuk is located on the Beaufort Sea in the western Arctic. The native people who live there are known as the Inuvialuit. Their name means "the people" in a dialect of the Inuit language called Inuvialuktun. People in Tuktoyaktuk are employed in a variety of jobs, though many still hunt during part of the year. Their homes are equipped with modern conveniences like those found in homes farther south.

Keeping tradition

With the modern lifestyle, many native people are concerned that they are losing the ways and skills of their ancestors. They feel that an important part of their heritage is hunting and fishing. Many residents of Tuk are eager to teach the traditional ways to their children. Native families have made a great effort to pass their native culture on to the younger generation.

Lucky plays with a husky pup.

The Pokiak family

The Pokiaks are one such family. They have made the decision to go back to using a dogsled instead of a snowmobile for hunting and are once again relying on the land and sea for much of their food. Randy is president of the Inuvialuit Development Corporation. Although he works at an office and travels south to meet with government officials, he still finds time to trap and hunt. In winter he hunts seals. In the fall migrating birds provide Randy and his family with extra food. The whale hunt, however, is the highlight of the year for the Pokiaks and many other families living in Tuktoyaktuk. As well as preserving a part of their cultural heritage, the hunt supplies the Pokiaks and other villagers with a major part of their winter food supply.

Before he leaves for the hunt, Randy says good-bye to his son, Enoch.

Tuktoyaktuk by night

Watching the weather

It is mid-July, and the weather is unusually cold and rainy. Strong winds whip up tall waves on the Beaufort Sea. Katie Pokiak keeps a careful eye on the weather. She knows that belugas migrate into shallower waters to calve during the summer. They only stay in waters near Tuk for about two months before heading out to deeper waters. There is not much time left! Katie and her husband Randy must hunt their whale soon. If they do not make a kill, they will not have their much-needed supply of meat and muktuk over the dark winter months.

Randy, whose nickname is Boogie, carves a caribou roast.

27

Instead of a kayak, Randy and Katie use an aluminum motorboat to hunt the beluga. With a kayak or umiak it would take a whole day to bring in a whale. With a motorboat and, using a gun, it only takes about two hours to bring in a whale.

The hunt begins

Early that afternoon Katie realizes that the wind has died down. Randy rushes to telephone his brother James and his uncle Steven. He wants James and Steven to hunt with them because whaling is always safer with two boats. They both agree to come.

Within a half hour the Pokiaks have said good-bye to their children, Enoch and Lucky, and are heading out to sea

in their small aluminum boat. Not too far from shore they meet up with James and Steven.

Randy and James each have handmade harpoons with strong metal tips. A bright red float on the end of a rope is tied to each tip. The two drivers steer the boats towards the hunting grounds. Suddenly Steven's experienced eyes spot a flash of white off his boat's starboard bow. It is a beluga surfacing for air.

Both guns and harpoons are used in the hunt.

The two boats chase the beluga for an hour, forcing it into shallow water.

Chasing the beluga

The two boats chase the beluga for almost an hour. The Pokiak's boat is closer to the whale, so Randy and Katie close in on the animal. They work together as a team. Randy stands in the bow of the boat, his rifle ready. Katie tries to keep the boat close to the whale so that Randy will be able to fire a shot into the whale's back. The whale continues to dive and swim in circles around the boat.

Then, suddenly, it is gone. Both drivers slow their motors and carefully look and listen. In a few minutes Katie spots the beluga in the distance behind them.

The drivers turn the boats around and start after the whale again. They know that the only way to catch the beluga is to drive it into shallow water. If they can chase the beluga towards the shoreline, it will not be able to dive too deeply. Between them, the two boats can force the whale close to shore.

The beluga starts to tire from the long chase. Soon Katie and Randy are within shooting range. Even though the waves have risen and are rocking the boat, Randy stands in the bow and aims his rifle as Katie moves the boat closer to the whale. When the whale surfaces, Randy pulls the trigger. The bullet hits the beluga.

Bringing in the whale

For a while the wounded beluga keeps swimming as it tries to escape from the boats but, finally, it is exhausted. It has to surface for air more and more often. As the boats pull up close to the whale, Randy and James stand in the bows with their harpoons. When the time is just right, they drive the harpoons into the whale's back. The whale keeps swimming and the ropes whir over the side carrying the floats. When the beluga comes up for air once more, Randy fires another shot. The red floats lie still on the water. The beluga is dead.

The dead beluga is tied to the boat.

James prepares to harpoon the wounded whale.

The whaling camp

James and Steven head for home. Katie and Randy tow the beluga to Hendrickson Island, where a whale-monitoring camp has been set up for the summer by a group from a Canadian university. A local Inuvialuit hunter named Jimmy Day runs the camp with the help of his family. The camp keeps a close eye on how many whales are being hunted in the area and what kinds of whales they are. Jimmy and his helpers check the species, size, age, and sex of each whale.

The whaling camp is busy. Jimmy Day and several other researchers are collecting information about the whales that have already been captured and brought to the camp that day. Katie and

Randy pull their whale alongside the other whales and speak briefly to the people studying and weighing the animals. Katie and Randy then walk up to the tents to exchange stories with some of the other whalers.

Soon it is time to leave the camp with their whale. The Pokiaks know that, with a dead whale in tow, it will take them a while to travel to the island near Tuk where they will cut up the beluga. By the time they arrive, it is ten o'clock, but it is still light out. The arctic sun does not set during the whole month of July.

Katie and Randy decide to get their children so that they can help with the butchering of the whale. They beach the beluga and head for home.

Susan Day has prepared a meal for her children, the researchers, and the whalers who come to the camp.

The whaling camp on Hendrickson Island.

Cutting up the beluga

By midnight the Pokiaks have returned with Lucky and Enoch. It is cold, and a steady drizzle is falling, but Randy is anxious to cut up the whale while the carcass is still warm. If he leaves it until morning, the whale will be stiff, cold, and difficult to cut.

Randy puts on hipwaders and walks into the shallow water beside the whale. With a sharp knife he cuts around the front flippers. He carries them to shore and then goes back to carve a line around the whale's neck. Then he cuts several straight lines from neck to tail, making wide strips of blubber. After each cut he peels back the blubber and separates it from the meat.

As Randy carries the strips of blubber to the beach, Katie and the children slice them into chunks and lay them on a platform of driftwood. They do the same with the strips of meat Randy has cut. The final job is to cut off the tail.

Even though the night is cold, and Randy has to keep plunging his hands into the icy water, he is able to keep them warm by holding them against the whale's warm insides. Nine hours after its heart has stopped beating, the dense layer of blubber is still keeping the whale's body warm. This shows how well insulated a whale is from the cold arctic water!

Before leaving the island for the night, the Pokiaks place plywood over the strips of meat and muktuk to protect them from hungry seagulls.

Randy makes a cut from the neck to the tail.

Randy warms his hands in the whale.

Time to go home

At two o'clock in the morning, twelve hours after the hunt began, the day's work is finally finished. Randy, Katie, and their children can finally go home and get some sleep!

Preparing the muktuk

The day after the hunt Randy and Katie return to the island with Lucky and Enoch. The Pokiaks want their children to learn how the meat and muktuk are prepared for the winter. Katie has also invited her sixty-five-year-old friend, Jean Keevik, to help cut up the muktuk. For helping the Pokiaks, she will be given some of the meat and muktuk. If Jean were to run out during the winter, Katie would happily give her more.

Jean and the Pokiaks cut up the muktuk and drop it into pails.

Randy and Katie build a simple table using driftwood and a piece of plywood. Lucky and Enoch play in the shallow water beside the whale carcass, pretending to be great hunters.

When the table is ready, the adults lift the plywood that covers the blubber. Then they pile the slabs of muktuk on the table and cut them into smaller pieces that fit into plastic pails. They peel the skin off some of the muktuk and put this blubber into other pails. Later this blubber will be melted into oil, or *ooksook*, and used to ferment the muktuk.

Jean slices the muktuk into strips.

A skillful cutter

Jean uses the *ulu* skillfully in the traditional style. She keeps the curved blade razor sharp by scraping it against a round stone or another knife blade. She is an expert at running the blade quickly along the lengths of muktuk and cutting very thin strips.

Jean sharpens her ulu on a stone.

Katie pops a piece of muktuk into her mouth. She likes the muktuk from the tail best.

Sampling the muktuk

Halfway through the day everyone takes a break to sit around the fire and taste some of the new muktuk. Using a sharp knife, Katie cuts some small pieces for her children before cutting up some of the tail for herself. They eat the muktuk raw with a little salt for seasoning. Everyone agrees that a snack of hot tea and muktuk is an excellent reward for all the hard work.

Boiled, fried, and fermented

The Pokiaks like raw muktuk, but they enjoy eating it in other ways. It also tastes good boiled, fried, and fermented. Fermenting muktuk is a favorite way of preparing this vitamin-rich delicacy. The muktuk is cut into large blocks and hung to dry for two or three days. Then it can be taken down and soaked in a bucket of ooksook for days, weeks, or months. The longer it ferments, the stronger its flavor. When it has turned to a light green color, it is perfectly aged.

Randy enjoys his muktuk with hot tea.

Jean starts cutting the meat.

A muktuk boil

Sometimes when muktuk has been dried in the sun for a couple of days, people go to the beach, build a driftwood bonfire, and have a muktuk boil! The muktuk is dropped into a large caldron of boiling sea water. After simmering for a couple of hours, it is eaten hot right out of the caldron or put in the refrigerator or freezer to be eaten later. Some families consider the flippers and tail to be the best muktuk and save these parts of the whale for Christmas dinner.

Lucky teases his parents by pretending he is going to put this huge piece of blubber into his mouth at once!

Cutting and drying the meat

After all the muktuk is cut and put in pails, work begins on the meat. Jean knows just how thinly the meat needs to be sliced so that it will dry evenly and quickly in the sun. It will spoil if it is left to dry too slowly.

When they have finished cutting the meat, Randy builds a sturdy drying rack using driftwood poles he has dragged up from the beach. The crosspieces are secured high enough that the meat will not touch the ground. Katie builds a smoky fire underneath to keep the flies away from the meat as it dries. Randy and Katie will have to return to the island several times over the next few days to keep the fire going and to turn the meat.

A smoky fire under the drying meat keeps the flies away.

Whale meat must be cut and hung properly to dry so that it does not spoil.

Randy covers the meat to protect it from rain.

Enough food for winter

When all the chores are finished, everyone piles into the boat and heads for the village. At home some of the muktuk will be put into the freezer for later that winter, and another portion will be left to ferment.

The Pokiaks are weary and cold after another hard day's work, but they feel happy that they have their whale and are prepared for the long winter ahead. Now they will have enough dried meat and muktuk to last till the next whaling season.

The unused parts of the whale carcass are left to drift out to sea.

Whaling for profit

Before there was electricity, people used candles and oil lamps for light in their homes. Streets were also lighted by oil lamps hung on poles. Great quantities of oil were needed, and the most plentiful and clean-burning supply came from whales. A whale's blubber could be melted down, or rendered, to form oil.

Before plastic and steel

Nowadays we can make metals and plastics that are flexible and strong, and we have many different uses for them. In earlier times the only material that was springy and yet would not break was whale baleen, or whalebone, as it was once called.

Many uses for whalebone

Whalebone was used for the springs in sofas, chairs, and carriages. People used it for fishing rods, the spokes of umbrellas, and even for stiffening fashionable clothes. As more and more uses were discovered for this springy material, bowheads and other baleen whales were hunted to a greater extent.

How it began

Hundreds of years ago the Basques of France and Spain went out in rowboats and harpooned the whales swimming close to shore. They were so skilled and successful that the whales in their area soon became scarce. The Basques were forced to travel farther north to find more whales. It did not take long for whalers to kill most of the whales in a particular area. As one species became scarce, the whalers moved to another region and hunted a different kind of whale.

By the 16th century the Basques, joined by the Dutch and the British, started hunting whales around Greenland. These whalers hunted the two most popular species of whale, the northern right whale and the Greenland right whale, also known as the bowhead.

Baleen was used to make many manufactured goods including carriage springs and umbrella rods.

A whaler's young helper stands baleen up to dry after it has been washed.

How the right whale got its name

Whalers called bowheads and the northern right whales "right whales" because they were the right whales to hunt. Their baleen is longer than the baleen of all other whales, and these animals possess very thick layers of blubber.

These two reasons alone would have made them the best whales to hunt, but right whales also offered another advantage. Their thick layers of blubber kept them afloat after they were killed. Other types of whales with less blubber sank when killed, and the whalers often lost their catch.

A bowhead's gigantic baleen.

The slaughter continues

Throughout the 18th and 19th centuries people discovered many new and varied uses for baleen and oil. As the demand for whale products grew, Europeans had to hunt more and more whales. Men were offered a lot of money to risk their lives on long, dangerous whaling journeys, but no one stopped to think of the consequences of killing so many whales!

By the 19th century Americans were also whaling in the western Arctic. Whaling was so profitable that whalers stayed in the Arctic over the winter too. Sometimes they were away from home for as long as three years!

Whaling ships were equipped with small boats that carried crews of five or more men. One directed the chase, another was the harpooner, and the rest of the sailors were oarsmen.

Whaling ships

The Basque, Dutch, and British whalers started building large sailing ships that could carry them to the arctic waters and had room for them to store their catch. They took smaller rowboats with them to use on board for chasing the whales. Six men went out in each small boat: four to row, an officer to steer, and the harpoonist at the front.

"Thar she blows!"

The lookout in the sailing ship spotted a whale by its "blow." He called out, "Thar she blows!" when he saw one, and the sailors quickly launched the two rowboats that hung at either side of the ship. No one spoke as they rowed towards the whale because whales have sharp hearing, and any noise might have frightened them away before the men were within harpooning range.

Braced for the kill

The harpoonist braced himself as he balanced the long, heavy harpoon. As soon as the whalers were close enough, the harpoonist hurled his weapon into the whale's broad, dark back. At once, in fright and pain, the whale dove. The strong rope attached to the harpoon uncoiled from the boat like a whip. The men had to be careful to stay clear of it. There were many tales of whalers getting entangled in the line and being pulled overboard to drown. As the whale swam to get away, it dragged the small boat with it at an alarming speed, sometimes for hours.

A blacksmith makes specialized whaling tools for use aboard the whaling ship.

"Thar she blows!"

The deadliest part

The most dangerous part of the whole hunt was killing the whale. The small boat had to draw alongside the tired whale so that the harpoonist could plunge the lance into its lungs. As soon as he had done so, the men had to row away with all their strength, for the enormous animal would rear up in a last effort to escape the pain. As the whale died, the giant flukes of its tail crashed down into the water. If the boat was too close, it was smashed to pieces, and the men often drowned.

A whaler stands on the carcass of a whale and cuts deep slices into its oil-rich blubber.

Flensing the whale

When the men in one boat caught a whale, the men in the other boat came to assist. Together the crew towed the dead whale back to the ship, which came closer to meet them. Once the whale was safely fastened alongside the ship, its carcass was stripped. The whale's head was cut off and hoisted up on deck. The baleen was cut out of the whale's mouth and was then cleaned, dried, and stored under the deck.

The whalers then put iron spurs on the soles of their boots. They leapt onto the floating whale and, with long-handled spades, started to cut it up. This process was called flensing. They began by cutting deep slices into the whale's skin and blubber. At the end of each slice they cut a hole and put in a large hook attached to a rope. When the whalers pulled on the rope, the skin and blubber peeled off the whale's body in strips. Once a whale was flensed, the carcass was allowed to drift away.

Wasted meat

Most of the whale's meat was wasted because the whalers could not store it on the boat. It would have spoiled by the time they reached home. Blubber, however, did not spoil and could either be stored for the return journey or rendered into oil. The rendering was done in large iron pots that were heated over a brick oven right on deck. Once the oil had cooled, it was kept in barrels below deck.

Crew members cut up a whale's fin and blubber on deck.

This whale, caught by Icelandic whalers, is being flensed in the old-fashioned way.

Technological advances

The whales that evaded the hunters for the longest time were the rorquals. Because they were so huge, and their layer of blubber was thin, these whales did not float when killed. Rorquals were also champion swimmers—too fast for whalers in their rowboats. By the middle of the 19th century, however, new inventions made it possible to hunt these whales too.

In 1859 the first steam-driven whaling ships were built. In 1864 the harpoon gun was invented. It was much more efficient than the old hand-thrown harpoon. The lance was replaced by a "bomb" gun, which instantly killed an exhausted whale. A hollow tube was then used to pump air into the dead whale so that it would not sink. These weapons made the hunt even more intense.

This whale did not have a chance of surviving in the face of modern whaling weapons!

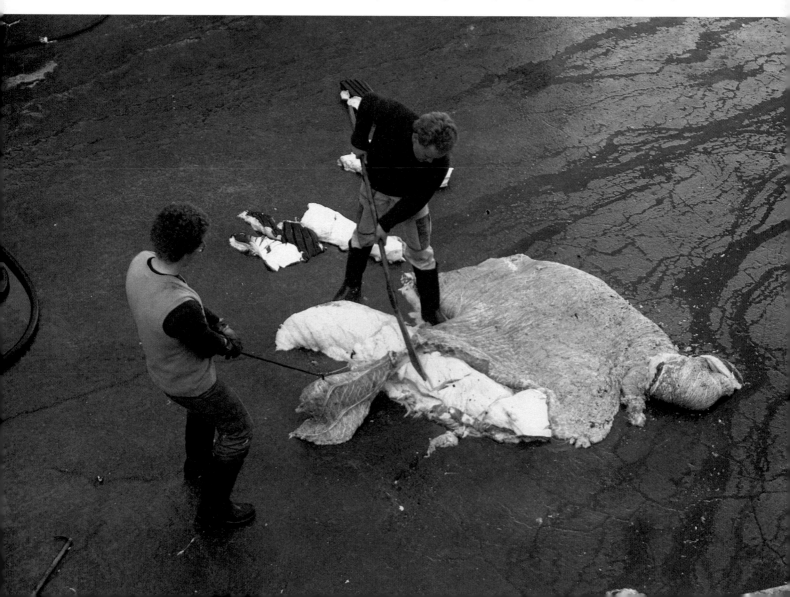

A whale has been hauled onto a factory ramp in Iceland.

Modern factory ships

Factory ships were first developed by the Norwegians. They were huge, floating processing plants. A whale was hauled up, sliced into pieces, and packaged into bundles of meat and blubber in under an hour! These factory ships killed more whales in a few years than other whalers did in hundreds of years. Because these ships were so expensive to operate, many whales had to be caught to make a single trip worthwhile.

A harpoon gun aboard a modern whaling ship.

Protection for whales

The whale is a magnificent creature—an intelligent mammal that humans have only lately begun to understand. Concerned people are now trying to protect and conserve whales and their environment.

Commercial hunting of whales is no longer permitted in the Arctic. Some local Inuit whaling is allowed to continue because many arctic communities still depend on whale meat and blubber. Many Inuit hunters are working together with conservationists in an effort to manage arctic wildlife. If proper care is taken to conserve wildlife, there will be enough whales to allow Inuit hunters to live and hunt in the traditional way as well as to ensure the survival of arctic whales.

A researcher at a monitoring camp checks the water for whales.

Monitoring camps

Because of the tremendous amount of overhunting that has occurred until quite recently, whale monitoring camps have been set up to keep a close watch on whale populations. These camps can be found all over the Arctic, where useful research on whales is being carried out. The people who work at the camps are interested in conserving whales. By watching, tagging, charting, and examining live and dead whales, they hope to discover how many whales of each kind there are. Studying whales helps northerners, government officials, scientists, and conservationists make decisions about which whales can be hunted and which must be protected.

The dangers of pollution

Whaling is not the only danger to whales. Sometimes whales collide with ocean-going ships or become entangled in fishing nets and drown. Oil-tanker traffic is very loud and disturbs the normal behavior of whales. Oil spills pollute the water and kill the marine life on which the whales feed.

Industrial pollution is one of the biggest dangers to whales. Toxic wastes that are dumped into river systems and oceans pollute the waters of the world. When the food on which the whales depend becomes contaminated, the whales soon become sick and die.

Belugas in danger

Although belugas in the St. Lawrence River have been protected since 1979, the beluga population has dropped from several thousand to just a few hundred! Toxic wastes in the Great Lakes river system are believed to be the cause. When one of these belugas dies, its carcass must be disposed of as toxic waste because it is filled with so many harmful substances.

You and your friends can help the beluga and all the living things that depend on the Great Lakes system by writing letters to the companies that are dumping toxic wastes into the water and to government officials, asking them to help stop the pollution. (See p. 57 for addresses.)

A whale thrashing in water after being harpooned.

A Greenpeace Zodiac tries to stop a whaling ship from hauling in a harpooned whale.

Conservation groups

The World Wildlife Fund and the Greenpeace Foundation are examples of conservation groups around the world that are trying to protect whales from extinction. Greenpeace is opposed to all whaling, while the World Wildlife Fund believes only carefully managed whaling should be allowed.

Scientific whaling

Many countries belong to an organization called the International Whaling Commission (IWC). Every year the IWC decides how many of each kind of whale can be hunted. Blue whales, right whales, gray whales, and humpbacks are officially protected by the IWC. However, many countries ignore the IWC's rules.

All the countries that belong to the IWC have agreed to stop commercial whaling by 1988. The IWC permits scientific whaling because scientists need to catch animals to study them. However, some countries continue to hunt hundreds of whales under the disguise of "scientific whaling" and then sell the meat in local markets. Most people believe that such abuse of scientific whaling permits should be stopped. Find out which countries are abusing scientific whaling and write to their governments asking them to stop.

Native whaling

Some conservation groups feel that no whaling should be allowed at all and have pressured native whalers to stop whaling altogether. Native peoples have always whaled in a responsible manner. They do not want to endanger the future of whales. Not only is the whale an important food source, but these people want to preserve their strong cultural tradition of whaling.

The number of whales caught by native peoples is monitored throughout the Arctic. Bowheads in the western Arctic are strictly limited; no bowheads are allowed to be hunted in the eastern Arctic. There are no strict limits on the belugas and narwhals.

For the Inuit of Greenland, the narwhal hunt is an important source of income. But it was feared that whalers with motorboats and guns had too much of an advantage over the narwhal and, before too long, it would be overhunted.

So the Greenland Inuit passed their own conservation laws. Now it is against the law to chase whales in motorboats; whales must be pursued from kayaks or umiaks, and they must be harpooned before being shot.

Conservation or starvation?

All over the world certain plants and animals are endangered. There are also people whose livelihoods depend on these plants and animals. Conservation groups around the world realize the importance of protecting endangered animals, but it is often difficult to make people give up one of their major sources of food or income.

Read the whaling issues carefully in this book and do some research on other animals or plants that are in danger of extinction. Have a debate on conservation and native survival issues with your friends. If you come up with some good solutions, write to your government representative or to a conservation group with your ideas. They will be happy to know you care!

Write a poem or song about whales

Write stories, poems, and songs about whales and draw pictures to go with them. Get your friends to do the same, and send these to a neighboring school. Ask the students at that school to do some whale projects, too, and to send them on to another school. Soon many students at many schools will care about whales, just as you do—and you will have made a difference to the cause of whales!

Glossary

baleen - Baleen consists of two horny plates attached to the roof of the whale's mouth. Each plate is made up of two to three hundred parallel slats with fringes that mat together to form a sieve for filtering food.

barnacles - Marine animals that are cemented to the bodies of larger sea creatures. Barnacles eat plankton which they catch with long, fragile legs called cirri.

blubber - Fat that lies between the skin and flesh of marine mammals. Blubber acts as a layer of insulation.

commercial whaling - Hunting whales for profit.

endangered - Very close to becoming extinct.

extinct - No longer alive or existing.

flensing - The process by which the whale's blubber is stripped from its body.

fluke - A whale's horizontal tail which is unsupported by bone.

Greenland - The largest island in the world located near the northeast portion of North America.

harpoon - A hunting weapon developed by the Inuit. The shaft was made out of bone or narwhal tusk and the tip out of walrus ivory or caribou antler.

International Whaling Commission - An international organization founded in 1946 to regulate the whaling industry.

Inuit - Natives of the Canadian Arctic and Greenland. This is also the general name for those who were formerly known as Eskimos.

Inupiat - The name given to North Slope Alaskan Inuit.

Inuvialuit - The Inuit who live on the Mackenzie Delta.

kayak - Developed by the Inuit, a kayak is a long, narrow, skin-covered boat propelled by a person using a double-bladed paddle.

krill - Shrimp-like marine animals that float freely in the ocean.

lance- A very long, slender whale hunting weapon used to make the final kill.

Mackenzie Delta - A low-lying plain situated in the western Arctic at the mouth of the Mackenzie River.

mammal - An animal that is warm-blooded, has a backbone and some form of body hair. A female mammal has mammary glands.

migration - Seasonal movements of animals that travel to chosen areas for feeding, breeding, or giving birth.

muktuk - Whale blubber with skin still attached.

ooksook - Blubber that is melted down to form an oil used in cooking.

plankton - Marine organisms that are eaten by larger animals—made up of tiny plants called phytoplankton and tiny animals called zooplankton.

pod - A small group of whales that travel together.

scientific whaling - Hunting whales for scientific study.

toxic waste - Unwanted material composed of substances that can, even in very small quantities, be a danger to health.

ulu - A sharp tool with a rounded blade used to separate blubber from skin.

umiak - A whaling boat large enough to hold eight people. It is open and has a wooden frame.

Yupik - The Inuit who live on the shores of the Bering Sea.

Acknowledgments

Cover photo: John Foster/Masterfile
Back cover photo: Ken Faris
Title page photo: Health and Welfare Canada
Photo credits: Ken Faris, pages 26-41, 52; John Foster/Masterfile, pages 20-21; Greenpeace/Deloffre, page 51(bottom); Greenpeace/Weyler, pages 53, 54; Barry Griffiths, pages 49(bottom), 50, 51(top); Health and Welfare Canada, pages 4-5; National Museum of Canada, pages 8, 9(bottom left), 9(bottom right), 10-11; Provincial Archives of British Columbia/78338, page 19(bottom); Public Archives Canada/C-30923, page 19(center), C-86450, page 48, C-23655, page 43(top); Public Archives Canada/Richard Harrington/PA 114686, page 19(top); Public Archives Canada/Walter Livingston-Learmonth/C-00212, page 43(bottom), C-88326, page 44, C-88268, page 45(bottom), C-88309, page 45(top), C-88347, page 49(top).

Illustrations: Brenda Clark, page 23; Lesley Fairfield, page 22; Karen Harrison, pages 6-7, 46-47; Susan Laurie-Bourque, pages 12-13; Elaine Macpherson, pages 9(top), 14, 16-17, 24-25.

Index

23456789 BP Printed in Canada 7654321098

Addresses for letter-writing activity on page 53:

In Canada write to:
The Minister of the Environment
House of Commons
Ottawa, Ontario K1A 0A6
Canada

In the United States write to:
EPA Administrator
401 M. Street S. W.
Washington, D.C. 20460
U.S.A.